Headline Series

No. 304   FOREIGN POLICY ASSOCIATION   Fall

Humanitarian Politics

by Larry Minear and Thomas G. Weiss

Cover Design: Ed Bohon $5.95

The Authors

LARRY MINEAR has worked on humanitarian and development issues since 1972, both as an official of Church World Service and Lutheran World Relief and as a consultant to UN organizations and the U.S. government. He currently codirects the Humanitarianism and War Project at Brown University's Thomas J. Watson Jr. Institute for International Studies.

THOMAS G. WEISS is associate director of Brown University's Thomas J. Watson Jr. Institute for International Studies and executive director of the Academic Council on the UN System. He has also held several UN posts, served as executive director of the International Peace Academy and written extensively about peacekeeping, humanitarian relief and international organizations.

Their recent joint publications include *Humanitarian Action in Times of War: A Handbook for Practitioners* (Rienner, 1993), *Humanitarianism Across Borders: Sustaining Civilians in Times of War* (Rienner, 1993) and *Mercy Under Fire: War and the Global Humanitarian Community* (Westview, 1995).

The Foreign Policy Association

The Foreign Policy Association is a private, nonprofit, nonpartisan educational organization. Its purpose is to stimulate wider interest and more effective participation in, and greater understanding of, world affairs among American citizens. Among its activities is the continuous publication, dating from 1935, of the HEADLINE SERIES. The authors are responsible for factual accuracy and for the views expressed. FPA itself takes no position on issues of U.S. foreign policy.

HEADLINE SERIES (ISSN 0017-8780) is published four times a year, Spring, Summer, Fall and Winter, by the Foreign Policy Association, Inc., 470 Park Avenue So., New York, N.Y. 10016. Chairman, Paul B. Ford; President, John Temple Swing; Editor in Chief, Nancy Hoepli-Phalon; Senior Editors, Ann R. Monjo and K.M. Rohan; Editorial Assistant, June Lee. Subscription rates, $20.00 for 4 issues; $35.00 for 8 issues; $50.00 for 12 issues. Single copy price $5.95; double issue $11.25. Discount 25% on 10 to 99 copies; 30% on 100 to 499; 35% on 500 and over. Payment must accompany all orders. Postage and handling: $2.50 for first copy; $.50 each additional copy. Second-class postage paid at New York, N.Y., and additional mailing offices. POSTMASTER: Send address changes to HEADLINE SERIES, Foreign Policy Association, 470 Park Avenue So., New York, N.Y. 10016. Copyright 1995 by Foreign Policy Association, Inc. Design by K.M. Rohan. Printed at Science Press, Ephrata, Pennsylvania. Fall 1993. Published April 1995.

Library of Congress Catalog Card No. 95-060107
ISBN 0-87124-162-5

Cover photo: *UNICEF*/93-BOU 1036/Betty Press. Authors' photos: Anita Fahrni.

Introduction

A STEADY STREAM of humanitarian crises, each of monumental and headline-capturing proportions, has assaulted the world's senses in the last few years:

- In the spring of 1991, following the Persian Gulf war, the plight of 1.5 million Kurds in the snowy mountains of northern Iraq dominated the news.

- Beginning in late 1991, the carnage, ethnic cleansing, systematic rape and forced movement of peoples accompanying the dissolution of Yugoslavia received major coverage. More than 4 million people were displaced and in need of international assistance for daily survival.

- Starting in mid-1992, famine resulting from Somalia's internecine warfare commanded world attention, with some half-million lives lost and the country's development set back for decades.

The authors acknowledge support for drafting this book from the U.S. Institute of Peace.

• In 1993–94, the distress of Haitians—fleeing in rickety ships from grinding poverty and major human-rights abuses in a country whose elected president was in exile—loomed large.

• In 1994, unthinkable butchery and massive displacement of Rwandans staggered belief. Half of the population of Rwanda was uprooted, with an estimated 500,000 to one million lives lost.

People in the United States remember not only the intense suffering of civilians caught in the crossfire and dramatized in the media. They also remember the U.S. response—sometimes timely, sometimes not; sometimes successful, sometimes not— to the plight of the needy. Etched indelibly in the national memory is the American-led operation to air-drop supplies to the Kurds and return them to their homes; the UN effort to reach people in Sarajevo and eastern Bosnia-Herzegovina (in the former Yugoslavia); the landing of U.S. troops in Mogadishu, Somalia, to protect aid operations; efforts to assist and protect people within Haiti and to rescue them on the high seas; and initiatives by humanitarian agencies and soldiers to assist injured and dying Rwandans.

Some of the images of rescues and rescuers evoke less positive feelings: the bodies of American soldiers being dragged through the streets of Mogadishu and one who survived being interrogated; the towering U.S. cargo ship *Harlan County* approaching Port-au-Prince, Haiti, and then retreating at the sight of armed thugs on the docks; the genocide in Bosnia-Herzegovina and in Rwanda, with Canadian peacekeepers under fire in the eastern enclaves of Bosnia-Herzegovina and the bodies of Belgian peacekeepers dismembered in Kigali, Rwanda's capital.

Other less-publicized recent tragedies—in Mozambique, Afghanistan, Sudan, Burundi, Liberia, Myanmar and East Timor—have also taken an enormous toll. In short, the decade of the 1990s is one of cataclysmic need that has sorely tested the strength of the global safety net.

What has changed in the early post-cold-war era is not the nature of the humanitarian enterprise. Desperate people still require relief supplies and protection from abuse of their fundamental human rights. What has changed are the political and military conditions that generate the need for humanitarian action.

Wars are different now. Virtually all of the recent humanitarian crises are the result of armed conflicts not between states but within states. Ruth Leger Sivard, chronicler of the world's annual military spending, reports in *World Military and Social Expenditures 1993* that each of the 29 conflicts claiming more than a thousand lives in 1992 were civil wars (see pages 6 and 7). In the most trying situations mentioned, humanitarian action took place in response to violent conflict within countries. One underlying cause of such wars has been that borders established in colonial days or as the result of the breakup of empires do not adequately take into account ethnic, tribal and religious factors.

Different Face of Civil War

Internal armed conflicts are more freewheeling than wars between nations that involve clearly identified protagonists, battle lines and ground rules. In civil wars, national authorities are challenged by one or more insurgent groups, equipped with weapons high-powered enough to wreak havoc but not powerful enough to secure victory. The mediation skills of the most sage tribal elder in Somalia or Afghanistan are likely to be outmatched by an AK-47 in the hands of a twelve-year-old.

Many weapon wielders—whether government or insurgent, organized military or ragtag paramilitary, or simply thugs—have little discipline, accountability, familiarity with applicable international law, or a perceived stake in negotiated solutions. Even when agreements are reached in negotiating capitals such as New York City and Geneva, Switzerland, there is little guarantee that dissidents within insurgent groups or subclans will respect them. Moreover, unchecked by traditional restraints and the discipline that normally characterizes professional armies, today's belligerents are more and more prone to using humanitarian assistance, and even civilian populations them-

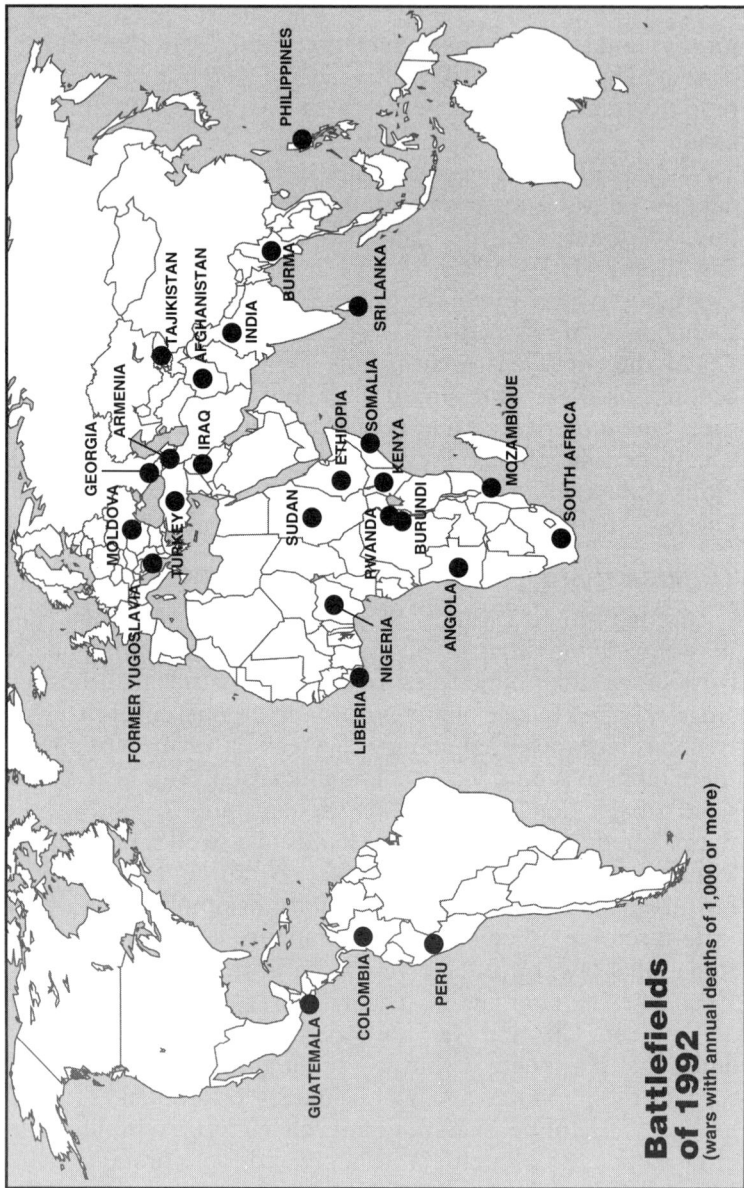

Battlefields of 1992
(wars with annual deaths of 1,000 or more)

Number of Wars and of War-Related Deaths

Deaths (in thousands)

Number of Wars

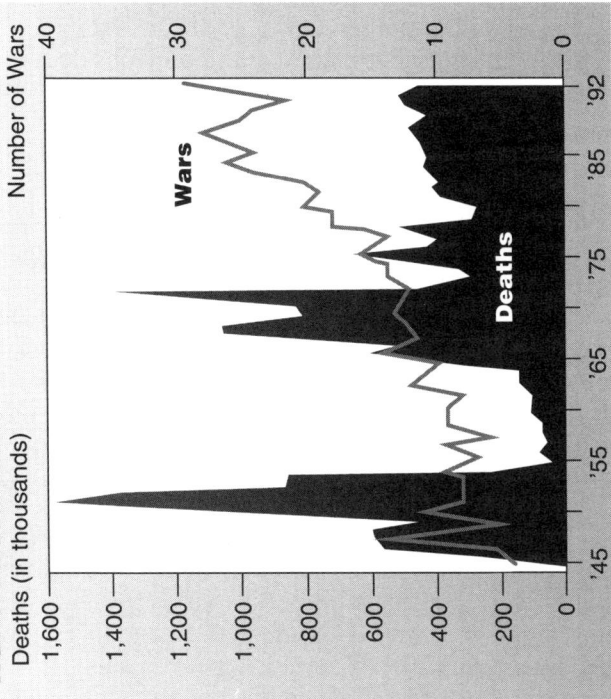

Countries indicated above

Afghanistan	Moldova
Angola	Mozambique
Armenia	Nigeria
Burma	Peru
Burundi	Philippines*
Colombia	Rwanda
Ethiopia	Somalia
Georgia*	South Africa
Guatemala	Sri Lanka
India	Sudan
Iraq	Tajikistan
Kenya	Turkey
Liberia	former Yugoslavia†

*Two wars in 1992
†Conflicts in both Bosnia and Croatia
Copyright © 1993 by World Priorities

Source: World Military and Social Expenditures, 1993 by Ruth Leger Sivard, Copyright © 1993 by World Priorities

selves, as weapons in their politico-military struggles. In many crises, humanitarian aid-givers are targeted for harassment and hostage-taking. Respect for aid personnel has plummeted.

The profusion of intrastate wars, with the 29 in 1992 representing an all-time high, conveys a misleading impression, however, of a whole new spate of conflicts. Many of today's armed conflicts are born of discontents that simmered during the cold war but were prevented from flaring into major conflagrations by the superpowers and their proxies. Although not widely realized, the cold war represented a humanitarian disaster of massive proportions for those whose suffering and abuse were overshadowed by the global sparring between the United States and the Soviet Union.

Though strife abounded during the cold war, there have been, in fact, more conflicts in the 1990s, and larger numbers of people imperiled by them, than in the previous decade. Those who had fled their countries for reasons of violence and persecution as of 1993 numbered some 18 million; an estimated 24 million people had been displaced within their own countries. "In a world population of 5.5 billion," reported UN High Commissioner for Refugees Sadako Ogata in her 1993 *State of the World's Refugees: The Challenge of Protection*, "roughly one in every 130 people on earth has been forced into flight."

Recent crises have been characterized by their quick onset and by the extraordinarily large numbers of persons affected. A day or two after Iraq's invasion of Kuwait in 1990, the first of an eventual 850,000 third-country nationals (mostly from poor Asian countries) appeared at the Jordanian border. Immediately after the plane crash in April 1994 that claimed the lives of the presidents of Rwanda and Burundi, hundreds of thousands of civilians were killed. In less than five days in July 1994, an estimated 1.5 million refugees had fled from Rwanda into Zaire; virtually overnight, a Detroit-sized city replaced the sleepy border town of Goma. Coping with such developments is beyond the capacity of existing aid mechanisms.

Economic factors have also made the humanitarian situation worse in recent years. While deep-seated ethnic tensions also affect populations in developed countries such as Northern Ireland, Canada and Spain, frictions are often far more unmanageable in developing countries. There, poverty is more prevalent, participation in the political process more limited, and mechanisms for the effective redress of grievances less well established.

Moreover, despite economic progress in selected countries and regions, the overall gap between the industrialized North and the less-developed South, in trade and investment as well as aid, has widened significantly during the past 10 years. As a result, poorer countries are more vulnerable to disruptive social tensions and less able to cope with them once they occur.

Changes in International Assistance

Twin trends in outside aid have contributed to the current spate of humanitarian crises. First, the level of international aid has fallen steadily for more than a decade. As a result, developing countries have had fewer resources to meet the basic human needs of their populations. Second, a larger share of the shrinking level of available resources has been diverted to emergencies. "Every year," observes Jessica Tuchman Mathews of the Council on Foreign Relations in a mid-1994 column in *The Washington Post*, "more money is spent on disaster relief, humanitarian assistance, refugees and peacekeeping: on keeping the awful from becoming worse. Less and less is left for making the bad lastingly better." According to recent statistics from the 25-nation Organization for Economic Cooperation and Development (OECD), 10 percent of all overseas development assistance in 1994 consisted of emergency relief; 20 percent of the latter went to one country, Rwanda.

Another major change concerns the understanding of sovereignty. Governments used to rely on their national sovereignty to serve as a cover behind which they could abuse their citizens with impunity. Given the destabilizing effects of such treatment on neighboring countries and entire regions, the UN Security Council has served notice on reprobate regimes—Iraq's President Saddam Hussein was the first to receive the message—that the treatment of civilians within established borders is no longer a purely domestic matter.

Similarly, providing humanitarian assistance in the past required the consent of the regime involved. In insisting on access to the Kurdish population in northern Iraq in early 1991 when the Iraqi regime opposed such action, the international community changed the rules of the game. In December of the same year, the UN General Assembly passed a resolution to the effect that the consent or request of a sovereign authority would no longer be required for the international community to gain access to distressed populations.

Complex Emergencies

War and weaponry, structural economic weaknesses and political volatility have joined to create a witches' brew called complex emergencies. Experts distinguish such emergencies from natural disasters. However formidable the task of responding to earthquakes, cyclones, droughts and floods, the challenges are largely logistical and technical in nature.

Complex emergencies, by contrast, occur as the result of the weakness or collapse of the state itself and the fraying of society, whether through insurgent challenge, economic and political disarray, or some combination of both. Mounting humanitarian responses involves not simply rebuilding a nation's housing or health system but reconstituting the fabric of civil institutions and reknitting the bonds of daily life. The challenge is Herculean, whether in hot-war situations in which rival political authorities vie for power or in postconflict settings where reconciliation confronts long-simmering grudges and unsettled scores.

Since "the humanitarian, political and security dimensions of [such] crises need to be faced in tandem," observed UN Secretary General Boutros Boutros-Ghali in a report to the General Assembly, "the task involves the international community in highly intrusive and political activities." It is, in short, impossible to tackle the human-needs agenda without taking political realities into account, and vice versa.

10

Changes in the international geopolitical climate, when combined with stresses and strains within countries, pose immense challenges for the world's humanitarian aid system. On the one hand, the proliferation of needs and the treacherous terrain on which they exist serve as a deterrent to humanitarian action. On the other, the erosion of national sovereignty and the advent of greater international concern and outrage heighten the pressure to act.

Governments, UN organizations and private relief agencies still remain the major sources of humanitarian aid. However, they, too, are evolving. Attempting to do more in the spirit of their humanitarian charters, they find themselves overwhelmed by the magnitude of needs and factors over which they have little control. Their efforts to function effectively on the highly politicized terrain of today's complex emergencies deserve both fuller understanding and critical review.

Chapter 1 examines prevailing understandings of humanitarianism and politics. Chapter 2 outlines the major actors in today's crises. Chapter 3 provides examples of different ways of responding to these crises, and Chapter 4 suggests changes in approach. In Chapter 5, the authors present challenges to U.S. policy.

The traditional view that humanitarianism and politics exist in two entirely separate spheres no longer reflects the real world. Hence the title of this book, "Humanitarian Politics." Based on a review of recent major crises, the book calls for a new, more nuanced understanding of the relationship between the two. It concludes that humanitarian action needs to be clearer about its possibilities and limitations while politics needs to be infused with humanitarian dimensions.

1

Humanitarianism and Politics

HUMANITARIAN ACTION, many believe, takes place unaffected by political factors in the countries that receive or provide aid and in the aid agencies themselves. Humanitarianism, after all, means helping people, irrespective of who they are, where they are located, and why they are in need. Rooted in morality and principle, such noble undertakings are also associated in some quarters with naïveté.

If humanitarian initiatives claim the moral high ground, politics would seem to occupy the low. Politics, "the art of the possible," is widely associated not with principle but with the compromise of principle. Politics is the arena where deals are cut, where campaign contributions buy access and the common good is ignored, where talk is cheap and tough decisions are deferred, where courage, integrity and resolve are in short supply.

Both humanitarian officials and politicians contribute to the stereotypes. Aid agencies go to great lengths to present themselves as nonpolitical and their motives as unalloyed. We have nothing to do with politics, private relief groups tell their contributors, who expect their contributions to be used exclusively for the direct alleviation of human need. "There is not a political bone in our body," the agencies in effect say.

In reality, humanitarian actors are deeply involved in the political sphere. To do their work, aid personnel and human-rights monitors usually require the permission of political authorities, which includes entry visas and residency permits. Relief programs need duty-free entry for supplies, permission to exchange foreign currency, and authority to communicate regularly and freely with their respective headquarters. Particularly essential—but also especially sensitive—in times of armed conflicts, aid agencies need access to distressed populations.

The day-to-day functioning of all aid agencies, whether private, governmental or UN, thus intersects in myriad ways with host governments and, in civil wars, with insurgent groups that act as the political authorities in the territories they control. Understanding the prevailing political environment is essential to successful humanitarian strategies.

Conversely, politics is the arena in which priorities are established, social contracts formed, participation and accountability nurtured. As the term "arena" suggests, politics is an ongoing struggle, within nations and between them. It commands constituencies by virtue of the vision that it promotes. Whether an issue is a domestic one such as abortion or an international one such as ethnic cleansing, political courses of action reflect understandings of shared values and responsibilities.

The question is not, therefore, whether humanitarian and political action intersect but rather how the interplay is understood and managed.

The Lay of the Land

As noted in the Introduction, the internal armed conflicts that dot the face of the post-cold-war world are highly political. Insurgent forces—sometimes large and well supported, sometimes small groups of thugs with narrow constituencies—

challenge the authority and legitimacy of established governments. In some civil wars, there are multiple challengers.

Not all modern belligerents lack humane visions or noble sentiments. Many have political platforms with praiseworthy aims. Moreover, many of the governments at war, and some of their adversaries, have publicly committed themselves to abide by international legal ground rules, which include conducting their fighting within stated limits and treating civilian populations humanely.

What happens in the real world, however, is something else again. A private group of luminaries, the Independent Commission on International Humanitarian Issues, concluded in its *Winning the Human Race?* that past experience has demonstrated that "as soon as they are directly or indirectly involved in an armed conflict, most states qualify, interpret or simply ignore the rules of humanity, evoking state interests and sovereign prerogatives." At such times, "Political considerations prevail over humanitarian requirements and humanitarian concerns are used to further political aims."

Access to civilian populations, despite being guaranteed by international law, is itself often a casualty of war. "When a man has placed his own life on the line and is prepared to kill or die for a cause," observes Francis Deng, a former diplomat familiar with the dynamics of war well beyond his own Sudan, "it is difficult for him to be overly concerned about the humanitarian needs of those who have remained behind enemy lines, especially if that would compromise the cause for which he has chosen to make the ultimate sacrifice."

In coming to the aid of civilians in places such as northern Iraq and Bosnia-Herzegovina, Somalia and Rwanda, therefore, the world walks directly into a political ambush. Warring parties can be expected to seek to employ outside aid to advance their various politico-military agendas. Politics in all likelihood will have played a role in creating the suffering, in framing the context within which outside assistance will be welcomed, and in influencing whatever outcomes emerge.

In addition, interventions to assist those in dire straits will

Patients at a medical facility operated by Médecins Sans Frontières (Doctors Without Borders) during the UN operation in Somalia.

themselves necessarily have political impacts. Even those agencies claiming to be apolitical will have to be politically astute. Denying the reality of politics will not cause politics to disappear, even for the most captivating or charismatic humanitarians.

Different Approaches

This treacherous terrain poses new and daunting challenges for humanitarian institutions. Many organizations are not anxious to get caught in political, much less military, crossfire. However compelling the claims of those who suffer, is it worth putting the lives of staff on the line or subjecting scarce resources to political manipulation and abuse? Accordingly, many agencies are rethinking the terms of their engagement in the new post-cold-war armed conflicts. Different groups are taking different approaches.

The world's preeminent relief agency in armed conflicts is the International Committee of the Red Cross (ICRC). It works tirelessly to insulate its activities both in theory and practice from politics. "Red Cross institutions must beware of politics as they would of poison," Jean Pictet has written in *The Fundamental Principles of the Red Cross*, "for it threatens their very lives." Like a swimmer, "in politics up to his neck...who advances in the water but who drowns if he swallows it, the ICRC must reckon with politics without becoming a part of it." Prominent among the ICRC's seven fundamental principles are neutrality (the refusal to take sides in hostilities) and impartiality (the nondiscriminatory and proportionate provision of aid).

Religious groups associated with social-justice traditions distinguish themselves from the ICRC's "charity" approach by affirming their partiality to, and solidarity with, the poor. "We do not identify with partisan causes. We identify with and respond to human needs," explains William Reimer of the Mennonite Central Committee, one of the U.S. relief groups that has reflected most deeply on such matters. "At the same time, we try to understand what the causes imply for the people. Each is legitimate, each has its own life."

Such varying philosophies produce highly different results in practice, even though the obstacles they confront are the same. The ICRC and others of similar orientation respond to needs, whatever their cause; their more justice-oriented counterparts take an active interest in addressing the root causes of suffering. The former are more insistent on gaining access to all sides before they will help any side. They mute public criticism of warring parties and factions that might make it more difficult to reach those in need. The latter, keen to be identified with the victims, are more willing to "go public" with their criticism of unacceptable actions by the authorities and to challenge whatever may be causing havoc. Beyond these two broad approaches, there are almost as many variations in understanding and managing the interplay of humanitarianism and politics as there are agencies.

In an effort to function more effectively in highly politicized situations, humanitarian organizations in recent years have given more thought to identifying and promoting the principles that shape their actions. The International Federation of Red

Cross and Red Crescent Societies in 1994 produced a set of guidelines for national societies and other interested agencies. The Mohonk Statement on Humanitarian Assistance in Complex Emergencies is based on a series of meetings held in the fall of 1993 under the auspices of the World Conference on Religion and Peace. The Providence Principles (see page 18), produced in 1993 by the authors of this HEADLINE SERIES under the auspices of the Humanitarianism and War Project at Brown University, are in wide circulation.

Some Ground Rules

Even though operating in highly politicized circumstances, humanitarian action does not have to be political. In fact, a guiding principle on which most organizations agree is that aid should not be denied to people who need it because they or their government are of a particular political ideology, economic philosophy, racial or ethnic makeup, or religious persuasion.

At the same time, effective humanitarian action needs to take into account a variety of political factors. Warring parties would like nothing better than to have an international humanitarian imprimatur on their cause and to enlist outside resources in their struggle. Organizations that wittingly or unwittingly allow themselves to be manipulated by warring parties lose their independence—an essential hallmark of humanitarian action.

Practitioners of humanitarian politics, therefore, must:

• pursue a firm commitment to principle, but also maintain a discerning eye for the most effective ways of putting principle into practice.

• nurture productive relationships with political authorities, but avoid compromising the integrity of their activities.

• expect manipulation by belligerents seeking to advance their own politico-military purposes, but find ways to preserve their freedom of humanitarian action.

• seek to maximize humanitarian benefits, but be aware of counterproductive impacts such as keeping the war alive.

• find ways of working with other humanitarian practitioners, but choose their partners with care.

Providence Principles of Humanitarian Action in Armed Conflicts

1. *Relieving life-threatening suffering:* Humanitarian action should be directed toward the relief of immediate, life-threatening suffering.

2. *Proportionality to need:* Humanitarian action should correspond to the degree of suffering, wherever it occurs. It should affirm the view that life is as precious in one part of the globe as another.

3. *Nonpartisanship:* Humanitarian action responds to human suffering because people are in need, not to advance political, sectarian, or other extraneous agendas. It should not take sides in conflicts.

4. *Independence:* In order to fulfill their mission, humanitarian organizations should be free of interference from home or host political authorities. Humanitarian space is essential for effective action.

5. *Accountability:* Humanitarian organizations should report fully on their activities to sponsors and beneficiaries. Humanitarianism should be transparent.

6. *Appropriateness:* Humanitarian action should be tailored to local circumstances and aim to enhance, not supplant, locally available resources.

7. *Contextualization:* Effective humanitarian action should encompass a comprehensive view of overall needs and of the impact of interventions. Encouraging respect for human rights and addressing the underlying causes of conflicts are essential elements.

8. *Subsidiarity of sovereignty:* Where humanitarianism and sovereignty clash, sovereignty should defer to the relief of life-threatening suffering.

Humanitarian challenges in today's highly politicized settings are producing changes within individual aid agencies and throughout the aid community as a whole. Some organizations are deciding against trying to deliver aid and protect human rights during active wars. Others are taking a closer look at how to do so with greater effect. Some are ordering flak jackets and armored vehicles and are providing their staff with security training and psychiatric help to deal with frontline traumas. Others are deciding to wait until the conflicts have subsided and social and economic reconstruction can be pursued more effectively.

A new concept of humanitarian politics is emerging. Humanitarianism is coming to be seen as requiring neither the denial of political realities nor their uncritical embrace. Humane values are best served by understanding and avoiding the manipulation inherent in armed conflict situations. For its part, politics is viewed as an arena that through domestic and international pressure can be made more hospitable to humanitarian action. Politics at its best embraces a vision of human solidarity and embodies a strategy for making that solidarity real.

2

Humanitarian
and Political Actors

THE HUMANITARIAN EMERGENCIES that confront the post-
cold-war world call to the stage two sets of actors. The first
are the institutions—governmental and nongovernmental, civilian and military—that provide relief assistance and protect
human rights. The second are the political players—the UN
system, governments, and insurgent groups—who frame the
context within which such humanitarian activities take place.
Some of the actors in each group come from outside the areas
of the conflicts; others, from the conflict areas themselves (see
opposite page).

External Humanitarian Actors

Key to the world's response mechanism is the UN system,
which includes several different humanitarian agencies staffed
by international civil servants. The four most central organizations with responsibilities in man-made emergencies are the
UN Children's Fund (UNICEF), the World Food Program

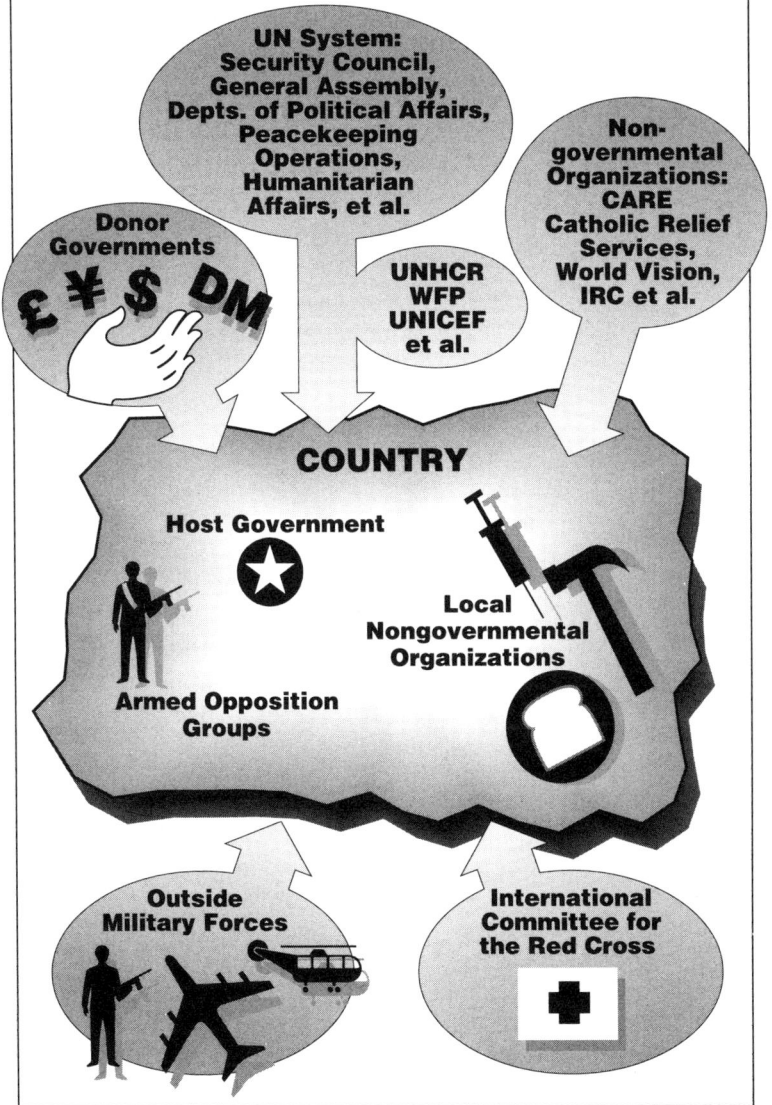

The Humanitarian Network
External and Internal Actors

UN System: Security Council, General Assembly, Depts. of Political Affairs, Peacekeeping Operations, Humanitarian Affairs, et al.

Non-governmental Organizations: CARE Catholic Relief Services, World Vision, IRC et al.

Donor Governments

£ ¥ $ DM

UNHCR WFP UNICEF et al.

COUNTRY

Host Government

Local Nongovernmental Organizations

Armed Opposition Groups

Outside Military Forces

International Committee for the Red Cross

Robert Mansfield

21

(WFP), the UN High Commissioner for Refugees (UNHCR), and the UN Center for Human Rights.

Since 1992, the UN Secretariat has coordinated the UN's humanitarian activities at the international level through the Department of Humanitarian Affairs (DHA). In crisis areas themselves, the coordination is usually handled by representatives of the UN Development Program (UNDP).

Experts differ about whether the world body should play a pivotal humanitarian role in civil wars. As a political organization comprised of governments, the UN has difficulty functioning in disputes involving member states. Through its decisions, for example, to impose economic boycotts or send military forces, the UN Security Council sometimes takes sides in a conflict, thereby complicating the efforts of UN humanitarian agencies to help civilians on all sides. As an organization of states, the UN also has an inherent bias against insurgent groups that challenge states. Moreover, UN humanitarian agencies are not necessarily suited to operate in active wars.

The governments that contribute resources to UN agencies and also operate their own bilateral programs are another major pillar in the world's humanitarian edifice. The U.S. Agency for International Development (AID) has traditionally been among the first to respond to major emergencies and frequently contributes between a third and a half of the total resources provided. European governments, in addition to having their own aid agencies, have contributed to humanitarian causes since 1992 through the European Community Humanitarian Office. While helpful, bilateral assistance is also more vulnerable to politicization than multilateral aid, whose multinational origins provide a certain protection against undue influence on the part of individual donors.

Private relief groups, or nongovernmental organizations (NGOs), constitute a third source of support. Numbering in the thousands, NGOs serve as channels for people-to-people contributions in emergencies. Some NGOs—for example, U.S. agencies such as Catholic Relief Services, World Vision, the International Rescue Committee (IRC) and CARE—expend as much in a given crisis as UN agencies or governments. Other NGOs make more modest contributions. Some NGOs mount a range of activities simultaneously in many crises; others concentrate their energies on a single continent (for example, Africa), crisis (Rwanda), sector (nutrition or health care), or population group (for example, orphans or refugees). Many NGOs have cultivated active and influential constituencies of private contributors.

NGOs Where Others Fear to Tread

NGO hallmarks are relatively low-overhead operations, quick response, and direct action (frequently on the front lines). They are also less bound by constraints of politics and sensitivities of sovereignty, often entering areas where governments and UN agencies fear to tread. Their staffs are highly motivated and unbureaucratic in approach, although their work sometimes suffers from a lack of coordination, follow-through and professionalism. While many in the United States view NGOs as a uniquely American phenomenon, they are in reality a feature of most developed countries, including those experiencing civil wars, as well as developing countries with active private sectors.

The International Committee of the Red Cross, founded in 1864 and based in Geneva, Switzerland, is in a category by itself. It has a mandate, conferred by international law, to assist and protect individuals in international conflicts and civil wars. Custodian of the Geneva Conventions of 1949 and Additional Protocols of 1977, the ICRC seeks to promote adherence to the rules of war and respect for the rights of civilian populations in wartime situations.

The ICRC's mandate thrusts it into all the world's major humanitarian crises. News reports rely on the ICRC, quoting "authoritative Red Cross estimates" of famine and displacement in places such as Kismaayo on the Somali coast, Gorazde in Bosnia-Herzegovina, and Kabul, the Afghan capital. ICRC staff are among the most intrepid, preceding the arrival of other agencies and the media and remaining in the line of fire after UN personnel, donor-government aid officials and even NGO field staff have been withdrawn. The ICRC 1993 budget, exceeding $500 million and funded largely by governments, paid the salaries of some 6,000 ICRC field staff, many hired locally.

Outside military forces are the fourth source of external humanitarian aid. Prior to the end of the cold war, foreign military personnel played a limited role in delivering humanitarian relief or protecting human rights. In the past few years, however, troops have been regularly pressed into such service. Beginning with the creation of "safe havens" for Iranian Kurds escaping Saddam Hussein's attacks in April 1991, outside military forces have become an important part of the international safety net for war-buffeted civilians. Operation Provide Comfort in northern Iraq was followed by the use of UN and U.S. troops in Somalia, UN troops in Croatia and Bosnia-Herzegovina and UN and French troops in Rwanda.

In each instance, the deployment of the military had positive results. Sometimes troops provided security, enabling traditional aid agencies to carry out their activities. The "heavy lifting" ability of troops to get large quantities of relief matériel to remote locations quickly is unexcelled. Sometimes military personnel themselves transported and distributed relief supplies.

Yet the use of the military has also been problematic. Military presence can be expensive, provocative and, from a local standpoint, overwhelming. Outside military forces can introduce a politicizing element. Furthermore, troops are often less willing to take risks than the aid personnel they are protecting, thereby limiting their usefulness. As a result, the utility of "military humanitarianism" has been seriously questioned.

To complicate the picture further, alternatives with no military component have sometimes not been very effective. The introduction of troops into Bosnia-Herzegovina or Somalia obviously did not provide adequate security for durable humanitarian operations. However, neither had the strategies tried before the deployment of soldiers. The world has yet to discover the proper mix of persuasion and military pressure in individualized situations to achieve humanitarian objectives.

By mid-1994, civil war had driven some 2 million Rwandan
refugees into neighboring countries. The UN provided a camp
for war orphans in Goma, Zaire, which gave shelter to one
of the largest concentrations of those who fled.

Local Humanitarian Actors

Turning to the actors within conflict areas, three deserve
mention. It may seem startling that the first two—governments
and insurgents—should be grouped among the humanitarians.
While the belligerents themselves create the overall conditions—and sometimes perpetrate the particular acts as well—
that require humanitarian action, they also have primary
responsibility for the health and welfare of their people. While
their pursuit of policies that savage individuals, groups and
entire civilian populations is well documented, governments
and insurgents also compete for the loyalty of people in areas
they seek to control and have a strong interest in seeing that
their basic needs are met.

In the Ethiopian civil wars of the 1980s, both the Ethiopian government and the armed opposition movements in Eritrea and Tigre sought to assist civilians. The government channeled assistance through its agriculture, labor and health ministries and Relief and Rehabilitation Commission. Its adversaries, the Eritrean People's Liberation Front and the Tigrean People's Liberation Front, had parallel ministries exercising similar duties and established relief associations to serve as channels for humanitarian resources from outside.

The governments of countries next door to conflicts often represent the front line in the world's humanitarian response. When workers from the Middle East, Asia and Africa fled Iraq and Kuwait after Iraq's invasion of Kuwait in 1990, it was the Jordanian government that first set up camps at the border to assist evacuees. Similarly, in the crisis in the Balkans from 1991 onward, the government of Croatia extended help to some 876,000 refugees and displaced persons, while the authorities in Serbia and Montenegro responded to the needs of almost 600,000. Interestingly, although ethnic tensions played a major role in such displacement, the hospitality extended was largely without regard to ethnic origin.

Private organizations, local leaders and the citizenry are a third and often undervalued humanitarian resource. In Amman, for example, residents of the Jordanian capital spontaneously gave food from their tables to the refugees from the Iraqi invasion of Kuwait. In Croatia and Serbia, more than 90 percent of those displaced by the conflicts were taken into private homes rather than refugee camps or holding centers. In both the Middle East and the Balkans, local Red Cross and Red Crescent societies took the lead in channeling assistance to host families.

Ethiopian famines have demonstrated the important role played by those most directly affected. In the famine resulting from the civil war in the 1980s, local people coped ingeniously with interference by the belligerents with nomadic migration patterns, the destruction of crops just prior to harvest, and the strafing of towns on market days. Communities organized self-help efforts and reached out to extended families and neighboring areas; people sold off household items and draft animals, before, as a last resort, migrating to population centers and relief camps. Even though in the end Ethiopians were overwhelmed by natural and human obstacles, the fact that they did not succumb sooner and at a greater cost of life was due primarily to local aid efforts. Local resources are often mobilized more quickly, provide more appropriate and cost-effective assistance, and have greater staying power than outside help.

Political Actors

The UN entities with political responsibility for humanitarian activities, in addition to the Security Council, the General Assembly and the secretary-general, are the Departments of Political Affairs and Peacekeeping Operations. The former monitors tensions around the world, carries out analyses of political hot spots, briefs the secretary-general, and provides staff support for UN efforts in diplomatic troubleshooting and conflict resolution. The latter implements Security Council decisions to establish, maintain and close down peacekeeping operations.

During the cold war, the Security Council generally responded to requests for an unarmed or lightly armed international presence only after the warring parties had consented. Subsequent UN operations have sometimes been deployed without the consent of the belligerents and with considerably more than the light arms of the past.

As of September 1994, the peacekeeping department was responsible for 17 operations involving some 72,000 military and civilian police personnel. Many of these were of a new-breed variety, reflecting what has been called the Dial 1-800-UN EPOCH. Peacekeepers have been dispatched to situations in which the government was ineffective (for example, in Rwanda) or even nonexistent (for example, in Somalia), often reinforced by civilian police and administrators, electoral experts, human-rights monitors and humanitarian personnel.

The local political authorities, governmental and insurgent, determine the prevailing ground rules for humanitarian action.

Somalia: Report from the Front

When I arrived in Mogadishu in mid-November 1992 to conduct interviews with aid agencies, the tension was palpable. The twin-engine ICRC plane from Nairobi, Kenya, was met on the tarmac by a bevy of aid staff and Land Rovers on hand to collect personnel and relief supplies. As the unloading proceeded, small-arms fire erupted near the runway. Unloading completed, the plane took off with the wind to avoid gunfire. Later incoming flights from Nairobi were diverted to a small landing strip an hour south of the capital.

I hitched a ride into the city with one of the aid agencies. We picked up an armed escort, and, before leaving the relative safety of the airport, my host gave the driver a fistful of currency in payment. Our Land Rover took us past blue-bereted UN peacekeepers from Pakistan, through the airport checkpoint and out into milling crowds of people and vehicles. At the aid agency, housed in its own walled compound topped with barbed wire and broken glass, the scene was one of pandemonium. Machine-gun-toting security guards opened the gates. The offices were jammed with people bustling about on various assignments. The air crackled with incoming and outgoing radio transmissions.

Conducting interviews in Mogadishu was an obstacle course. Just getting from one session to the next meant lining up a vehicle and driver, arranging for an armed escort, and confirming departures and arrivals by two-way radio. The difficulties paled in comparison with the challenge of carrying out humanitarian activities. The priority was to get food and medical supplies to people in the capital and in outlying areas to reduce the death rate due to starvation and disease. At the height of the crisis, deaths in Baydhabo, Somalia, alone were estimated at 800 to 900 per day.

During my visit, I stayed with aid personnel—the principal hotels were a casualty of the violence—and attended their meetings. Unlike the stereotypical aid people—international ambulance chasers bent on making the daily CNN Mogadishu feed—they were serious professionals struggling with how to help civilians caught in the crossfire of a civil war. They agonized about whether to give in to the

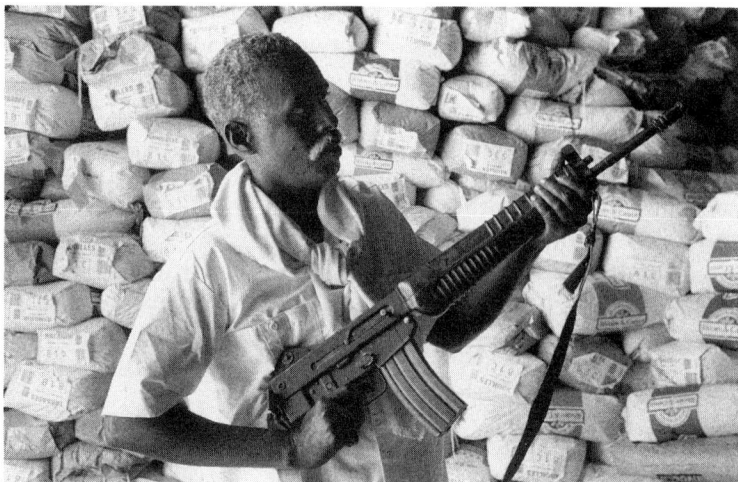

A guard watches over a warehouse full of relief supplies in
Mogadishu, Somalia, in September 1992.

*extortion demanded by "technicals," the security guards who came
with the vehicles they hired; whether to take action, and if so what
action, to reduce leakage of supplies through pilferage and ripoffs;
whether to risk injury to staff by continuing programs in insecure
areas; and whether, given all of the above, to curtail or suspend
activities altogether.*

*One particularly divisive issue concerned additional outside
military protection for relief operations. A score of U.S. aid groups
in November wrote the U.S. national security adviser requesting
greater protection than the UN peacekeeping troops on the scene were
able to provide. Their action was criticized by other relief organizations and the UN peacekeepers who feared additional military
personnel would escalate, rather than contain, the existing violence.
Two weeks later, U.S. troops landed to protect aid activities. The
rest is history.*

Larry Minear
December 1992

In the former Yugoslavia, for example, the Bosnian Serbs, whose political and military objective was to isolate or expel Muslims, tightly controlled international access to them. Even when a regime or insurgency is headed by civilians, military and paramilitary forces often wield disproportionate power and authority. Lacking accountability to their citizens or the international community, they make it difficult for humanitarian institutions to function.

The relative power and influence of local institutions—civilian and military, public and private—thus have a major bearing on humanitarian activities. Foreign and local humanitarians, if they are to succeed, must take into account the orientation, objectives and resources of these local groups.

Other Actors

Foremost among the other actors who influence humanitarian activities are the media. The media's capacity to affect foreign policy is not new. Before the Spanish-American War of 1898, for example, William Randolph Hearst, the newspaper magnate, commented to Frederic Remington, the artist: "You furnish the pictures; I'll furnish the war."

More recently, the media have played a role in galvanizing international help for victims of civil wars in Biafra, Nigeria's secessionist state, in the 1960s, in Bangladesh (formerly East Pakistan) in the early 1970s, and in Ethiopia in 1974 and again in 1984. Media influence has increased in the post-cold-war period. U.S. Ambassador to the UN Madeleine K. Albright refers to the media as "the 16th member of the Security Council." Other observers have quipped that when it has come to influencing international responses to crises in Kuwait, Somalia, Bosnia-Herzegovina and Rwanda, Ted Turner and his Cable News Network (CNN) rather than the UN secretary-general or the U.S. President have often been in charge.

The media have had both positive and negative effects. In Somalia, the coverage of famine and war mobilized international concern. Dramatic images of U.S. troops arriving on the beach in Mogadishu helped deepen American interest, involvement and aid. Yet television coverage of the killings of U.S. Marines by local Somalis played a role in accelerating the withdrawal of U.S. and other troops.

In addition to dramatizing needs, stimulating action, mobilizing resources and publicizing abuse, the media have played a role in generating the wrong kinds of assistance and the skewing of allocations of resources and personnel among geographical areas. The media have often ignored the role and contributions of local people and local humanitarian institutions, highlighted the perceived bungling of aid groups, and given inadequate attention to political and other factors that are essential for understanding what is taking place.

Prominent individuals, acting in their personal capacities, have also played important roles. Former President Jimmy Carter, for example, had helped mediate political differences in Sudan and Liberia before his more publicized recent efforts in Haiti and Bosnia-Herzegovina. British rock performer Bob Geldof raised public awareness of the famine in Ethiopia in 1984 through concerts and raised funds for the starving. UNICEF goodwill ambassadors such as Liv Ullman and the late Audrey Hepburn have mobilized support for efforts to improve the condition of women and children.

Conclusion

Although the dynamics of humanitarian crises vary, the same groups of players respond to each crisis. None of the actors is completely satisfied with its performance; each is reviewing recent activities and rethinking approaches. Time-tested assumptions about the respective roles of the UN and private relief groups, for example, and about the relationships between humanitarian and political actors are receiving fresh scrutiny. The following chapter explores how these various actors interact as the international community responds to particular crises.

3

Getting the Relationship Right

T HERE ARE SEVERAL APPROACHES to managing the inevitable tensions between humanitarianism and politics. The first subordinates humanitarian action to politics, as a review of the experience in Nicaragua during the 1980s demonstrates. The second elevates humanitarian action above politics, as has been the case in the former Yugoslavia.

The third approach places humanitarian and political action on parallel but separate tracks. In this approach, humanitarian efforts help to create a climate in which durable political solutions may be found but these efforts are not made subservient to political considerations.

Humanitarianism Subordinated to Political Goals

The politicization of the humanitarian enterprise is seen most clearly in the policies followed by the United States and the Soviet Union during the cold war. The political and economic confrontation between the two superpowers played itself out not only in their relations with each other but also through their actions in developing countries around the world. Under the "Reagan doctrine" of supporting anti-Communist insurgencies, the United States backed antigovernment forces in Afghanistan, Nicaragua, Angola and Cambodia; comparable Soviet policy in the form of the "Brezhnev doctrine" justified Soviet intervention whenever a Communist regime was threatened.

As a result of the Reagan doctrine, the United States reduced short-term emergency and longer-term development aid to countries not victims of Communist insurgencies and with limited strategic importance for the United States. Since the United States was the largest contributor to UN humanitarian agencies and a major supporter of private relief groups, the entire humanitarian apparatus suffered.

▶ **The Case of Nicaragua:** A review of U.S. policy toward Nicaragua in the 1980s illustrates the extent to which humanitarian assistance was pressed into the service of political objectives. The Reagan Administration viewed the Sandinist regime, a Communist government with links to Fidel Castro's Cuba and to revolutionary movements in El Salvador and Guatemala, as a threat to the United States. U.S. policy accordingly supported the contras, a Nicaraguan politico-military insurgency committed to the regime's overthrow.

U.S. support included weapons and training for the contra military provided by the Pentagon and the Central Intelligence Agency (CIA) and financial underwriting by the State Department and AID. In 1985, Washington imposed an embargo on trade with Nicaragua, although it exempted humanitarian items. The Administration requested, and the U.S. Congress provided, $27 million in "humanitarian assistance for the contras," including boots, tents and telecommunications gear. In 1986 the State Department considered declaring the politico-military arm of the contras, the United Nicaraguan Opposition, a "private and voluntary organization" so that it could receive U.S. food and other government aid available only to bona fide humanitarian relief agencies.

In later judicial proceedings, two U.S. officials pleaded guilty to criminal charges of conspiracy to defraud the U.S. government by encouraging charitable tax-deductible contributions to private organizations that would be used to support contra military activities. Meanwhile, legitimate emergency assistance from AID flowed to private relief groups working with Nicaraguan refugees who had fled into neighboring countries. However, such aid was denied to agencies seeking to meet urgent humanitarian needs within Nicaragua itself. In 1988 the same Administration that had included jeeps in its contra aid shipments prevented privately collected humanitarian items from leaving Texas bound for Nicaragua aboard what the press described as "mostly small pickup trucks, aging school buses and rickety, brightly painted panel trucks."

Because such events were part of the larger geopolitical struggle, they were the subject of daily media coverage and public discussion. "Humanitarian assistance," used very loosely, became a household word. "Anyone who examines the historical record of communism must conclude," declared *The Washington Times* in a May 10, 1985, editorial, "that any aid directed at overthrowing communism is humanitarian aid." Largely unheard amid the clamor were the voices of a few lone U.S. private relief groups who protested the abuse of the concept and warned that legitimate humanitarian activities and personnel in the region were imperiled as a result.

The World Court in 1986, finding against the United States in a case brought by Nicaragua, affirmed that authentic humanitarian assistance "makes no discrimination as to nationality, race, religious beliefs, class or political opinions. It endeavors only to relieve suffering, giving priority to the most urgent cases of distress." Washington, which rejected the compulsory jurisdiction of the World Court in the matter, also ignored its finding.

With the passing of the cold war, humanitarian assistance was no longer subordinated to an anti-Communist political agenda. Yet patterns established over more than 40 years die hard. The United States recently extended its economic embargo on Cuba, which, despite an exemption for humanitarian items, has worked great hardship on the health and well-being of the island's people. There have also been calls for "a new extended cold war" against the Serbs, a strategy with negative implications for humanitarian assistance to the needy in Serbia.

Meanwhile, the true character of the aid supplied by the other side in the East-West struggle has also been exposed. Once an enthusiastic donor of both military and development aid, the former Soviet Union has all but abandoned its earlier aid activities. Soviet-bloc countries that previously helped Vietnam, for example, halted such aid after the fall of communism. Assistance to Soviet clients in Afghanistan and Cambodia has similarly dried up.

Many expected that with the end of the cold war, politics would play less of a role in the U.S. response to life-threatening suffering. Instead, humanitarian action has been subordinated to a new set of political factors. Humanitarian assistance now carries economic and political messages, such as the promotion of multiparty democracies or free-market economies.

Other Pressures

American politics and public opinion also continue to influence U.S. humanitarian action. At a time when the UN and its member states are increasingly beset by complex civil wars, the political, economic and military pressures on Washington and other Western capitals to avoid engagement are growing. Presidential Decision Directive (PDD) 25, unveiled in May 1994, reflects this reticence and represents a 180-degree policy reversal by President Bill Clinton from the "assertive multilateralism" articulated in his 1992 campaign and at the outset of his Administration.

Only three years separated the bullish idealism reflected in the U.S. policy guaranteeing survival to the Kurds in northern Iraq and the utter cynicism of a policy that ignored Rwanda's unfolding tragedy. Over roughly the same period, the U.S. approach to the former Yugoslavia has been one of firmness at the level of rhetoric but hesitation on matters of actual engagement. The impact of U.S. vacillation on the UN system has been profound since U.S. participation remains, for the time being at least, essential to UN initiatives, especially those involving significant military forces.

PDD 25 spells out strict conditions to be met before the United States agrees to participate in any UN operation. These include a clear statement of American interests, the availability of troops and funds, the approval of the Congress, a specific date for U.S. withdrawal, and appropriate command and control arrangements. Washington will block any new UN operations, even ones without U.S. soldiers, unless its criteria are satisfied.

Since new and urgent needs will rarely, if ever, satisfy these political conditions, the effect of Washington's policy is to place severe limits on humanitarian initiatives. "You have to question whether a humanitarian imperative constitutes a vital interest," retired U.S. Marine General Bernard E. Trainor has observed. "One would like to use the doctrine of limited tears," he says, capturing the spirit of PDD 25 nicely. "We can't cry for everyone, so we should have some measure that helps us to decide where and when to get involved."

In sum, making the delivery of relief supplies or the protection of human rights subservient to political objectives or conditionality damages the integrity of humanitarian action. Humanitarianism viewed as an extension of politics by other means, to paraphrase the Prussian military strategist Karl von Clausewitz, is not authentically humanitarian, whatever the character of the politics.

Cure-all Humanitarianism

Another approach makes humanitarianism a substitute for attacking the root causes of violence. Confronted by a world in which armed conflicts proliferate, refugees abound and human-rights abuses are legion, the international community often puts its energies primarily or exclusively into efforts to assist the victims. This approach asks too much of humanitarian action.

The promoters of what could be dubbed cure-all humanitarianism are often the humanitarian organizations themselves. Their single-minded preoccupation with the relief of suffering sometimes leads them to approach emergencies in a political vacuum. "URGENT...URGENT...URGENT...URGENT ...URGENT...URGENT," proclaims a 3.5 x 7-inch mail solicitation appealing for funds for Rwanda and Haiti. "Your gift is urgently needed today to provide relief and supplies to desperately poor children and families." The 100-word appeal concludes with the peroration, "It is easy to CARE—please send your donation today. Thank you."

Politicians, too, are well-known promoters of humanitarian hyperactivity. Unable to agree on diplomatic or military steps needed to deal with complex problems, they often embrace aid as a less controversial and less politically costly strategy. The world's response to the conflicts in the former Yugoslavia provides an apt illustration.

▶ The Case of Yugoslavia: Since the fall of 1991, the UN Security Council has passed more than 50 resolutions dealing with the breakup of Yugoslavia and the wars that followed. It imposed and then tightened an embargo on deliveries of weapons and military equipment; committed UN peacekeeping forces and associated personnel to Croatia, Bosnia-Herzegovina and finally Macedonia; decried ethnic cleansing and other human-rights abuses; endorsed expanded humanitarian-assistance activities; and approved "all measures necessary" by member states to assure that humanitarian personnel have access to civilians.

As the war has ground on, economic sanctions and peacekeeping have bogged down, a political settlement has proved elusive, and differences among key Security Council members have widened. Humanitarian matters have accordingly loomed larger and larger in the council's actions. The creation of "safe areas" in eastern Bosnia-Herzegovina became emblematic of commitments made in New York City, undertaken in the full knowledge that they would make little difference on the ground. Aid personnel in the region use the shorthand term "humanitarian alibi" to refer to Security Council measures taken so that governments could appear to be doing something without really doing anything at all.

Violence in the Balkans

In September 1993, I returned to Zagreb, now the capital of Croatia and the site of a wonderful vacation many years ago. I had gone there to complete the fieldwork for a case study on the plight of the former Yugoslavia for the Humanitarianism and War Project. Only Air Croatia was flying, and the route was indirect to avoid infringing upon the sovereignty of Serbia. The state-of-the-art airport, complete with digital displays and videos, gave little clue of the scenes to come. The first indicator of the war's presence was the traffic jam beside the hotel, caused by the fleet of white UN Protection Force vehicles, the dominant humanitarian presence in Zagreb.

A journey the next day to the Bihac "pocket"—a landlocked Muslim enclave in Serbian-occupied Bosnia—provided a glimpse into the madness that had become the Balkans. To visit this area a mere 75 kilometers away required traveling six hours along a deserted macadam road that had deteriorated because of the war and lack of maintenance. Equipped with helmet and flak jacket, I sat in the cab of a German-built truck with a jovial driver from the

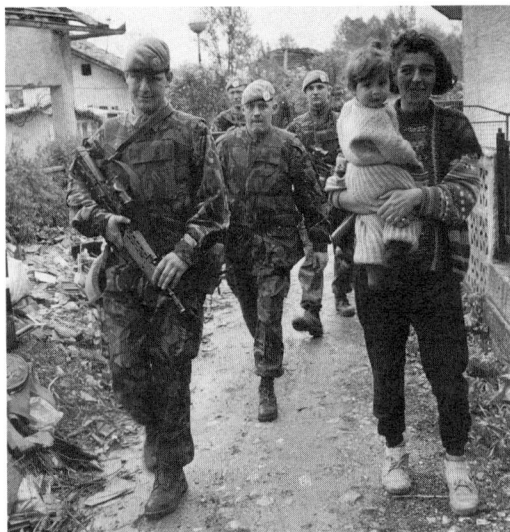

UN soldiers of the British Battalion on patrol in the Muslim enclave of Stari Vitez, Bosnia-Herzegovina, in May 1994.

Danish Refugee Council project, which was under contract with the UNHCR. Our 10-truck convoy went through 14 checkpoints before reaching Bihac. Bihac citizens depended on the daily delivery of food from such convoys. Yet, the traffic was routinely stopped by a motley assortment of troops—some in uniform, others not—from Croatia and the Serb-controlled krajina, various militias and local police, and UN soldiers from such far-off places as Fiji.

The devastation of the villages in Bihac was particularly unsettling because it was not the result of bombs dropped anonymously from high altitudes but the work of individuals—neighbors using explosives to destroy each other's houses and mosques. This same "homemade" quality of violence provided an insight into the concentration camps, sniping, rape and mortars lobbed at markets.

At the time Bihac's security was guaranteed because Fikret Abdic, its major entrepreneur, had managed to cut a deal with all of the key players—Serbs, Croats and Muslims. A French UN peacekeeping battalion monitored the scene; the deutsche mark was the currency.

In December 1994 Bihac was back in the news. This time the Bosnian government's army sought to retake it from the Abdic forces. This war, within the larger war, pitted Bosnian Muslims against Bosnian Muslims. Retaliation, first from Sarajevo authorities and then from the krajina Serbs, was swift and severe. The latter used bombers and soldiers who had managed to secure arms despite the international embargo.

Hearing of the December events, I recalled a conversation with a colleague and friend who had spent much of the war in Sarajevo: "If the UN had been around in 1939," he said, "we would all be speaking German." Whether speaking of military, humanitarian, human-rights or diplomatic efforts, collective spinelessness rather than collective security had characterized the international community's approaches.

Thomas G. Weiss
December 1994

39

In the case of Yugoslavia, politicians rather than aid organizations resorted to cure-all humanitarianism. In fact, many humanitarian groups throughout the crisis have appealed to governments to address the underlying causes of the mayhem, which they term "a humanitarian problem without a humanitarian solution." The Soros Humanitarian Fund for Bosnia-Herzegovina took out a full-page ad in major newspapers in April 1993 to convey its support for more decisive action. "We have become convinced that humanitarian aid without adequate political and military action against the Serbian aggressors is not effective," the signers wrote in an open letter to President Clinton. They recommended "a credible deterrent" to protect Muslim areas, including aircraft "to attack artillery units which are firing on those enclaves or on humanitarian convoys."

Despite efforts to bring political, diplomatic and even military pressure to bear on the belligerents in the Balkans, humanitarian assistance over time became the focal point of international activity. Initially, humanitarian activities were mounted to buy time for political solutions, to "reverse the logic of war," as aid officials explained. But the war resisted international efforts at resolution, and humanitarian activities became, for all practical purposes, an end in themselves.

A succession of negotiated settlements failed to win the agreement of the protagonists, while other governments and the UN remained divided about the appropriate mix of political persuasion, economic sanctions and military force. Governments that could not agree on whether to use military force against the Bosnian Serb army or whether to lift the arms embargo against the Bosnian government emphasized their agreement on humanitarian aid, to the evident discomfort of aid practitioners. "It is not simply that the UN's humanitarian efforts have become politicized," observed a senior UNHCR official ruefully in late 1993. "It is rather that we've been transformed into the only manifestation of international political will."

The UNHCR was criticized for both malfeasance and nonfeasance: that is, for moving people out of harm's way, thereby

UNHCR Ogata on an inspection visit to Sarajevo, Bosnia-Herzegovina, July 1993.

UNHCR

contributing to ethnic cleansing, and for failing to reach them and protect them where they were. As High Commissioner for Refugees Ogata queried: "To what extent do we persuade people to remain where they are, when that could well jeopardize their lives and liberties? On the other hand, if we help them to move, do we not become an accomplice to 'ethnic cleansing'?" The dilemma was complicated by the broader failure of governments to take the necessary political steps to stop the bloodshed. UN agencies were criticized for not being assertive enough in rescuing people when, in part, they were being pressured to spare European governments from having to grant asylum to the ethnic-cleansing victims who might indeed have been brought to safety.

Private agencies, too, felt compromised by the lack of political action. "People look at us as if to say, 'We know you're feeding us to compensate for the fact that your governments won't act,'" observed a Sarajevo-based relief worker with a private French agency. Other aid personnel, too, suspected that they were not taken seriously by the warring parties. NGOs and UN personnel came to think of their work as constituting a "humanitarian fig leaf," and a rather transparent one at that.

The recurrent interruption of relief activities and the continual harassment of aid personnel by the Bosnian Serbs suggested a cold calculation on their part. They were banking on the fact that the international community could be counted on to insist on maintaining the humanitarian alibi at virtually any cost. Aid agencies, given their interest in helping people, had difficulty in suspending or terminating relief operations, even when the effectiveness of such activities had been compromised.

At the end of the day, humanitarianism as a substitute for other action is doomed. In the former Yugoslavia, aid agencies fought a losing battle to stanch the suffering generated by the failure of peacemaking efforts. Humanitarian workers and political leaders alike conceded the problem. "We have chosen to respond to major unlawful violence," concluded veteran UN-watcher Rosalyn Higgins, "not by stopping that violence, but by trying to provide relief to the suffering. But our choice of policy allows the suffering to continue."

Thus, humanitarian action pursued in a vacuum sustains conflicts. It allows aid resources to be appropriated by belligerents and eases the burden of caring for their respective populations. It plays into war strategies by opening up roads and stimulating an aid-cum-war economy. That experience in the former Yugoslavia is similar to difficulties in Sudan, Ethiopia and Sri Lanka. Humanitarian action undertaken without regard for political realities is ultimately self-defeating.

Humanitarianism in Partnership with Political Action

The third approach seeks to avoid the pitfalls of humanitarianism that is subservient to political goals, on the one hand, or a substitute for political undertakings, on the other. It views humanitarian and political action as each important in its own right and, if properly managed, mutually reinforcing. The image of "parallel tracks" conveys both the connection as well as the separation necessary for the association to be effective.

Two illustrations demonstrate a failure to get the relationships between humanitarian and political goals right: the economic embargo of Haiti (1992–94) and the aid operation in Sudan in the early 1990s. Two contrasting examples of successful humanitarian and political interface are drawn from recent UN initiatives in Cambodia and El Salvador.

In an effort to pressure the Haitian military regime of Lieutenant General Raoul Cédras to step down and restore to power the elected president, Reverend Jean-Bertrand Aristide, the UN Security Council imposed increasingly harsh economic sanctions. These measures worsened the living conditions of the vast majority of the poverty-stricken population of the Western Hemisphere's poorest country yet failed to alter the policies of the junta. The suffering caused by UN-sanctioned deprivation was greater than the relief provided by UN and other humanitarian activities. Tens of thousands of Haitians chose flight in unseaworthy small craft rather than face suffering and repression at home.

In July 1994, the Clinton Administration, responding to public pressures, sought and received Security Council approval for a U.S.-led military invasion under Chapter VII of the UN Charter to restore the elected government. In last minute negotiations conducted by former U.S. President Jimmy Carter, the junta consented to the arrival of armed military personnel and the restoration of the country's elected president. Had an invasion been carried out in 1992 instead of 1994, disastrous consequences for the well-being of the civilian population might have been avoided. As it was, humanitarian considerations were subordinated to an ineffective politico-military strategy.

Operation Lifeline Sudan was a pioneering venture that broke new humanitarian ground. The UN persuaded the protagonists in the civil war to provide access for international personnel to the civilians in areas they controlled. Launched in April 1989, Lifeline negotiated corridors of tranquillity for an effective relief operation by road, river and air across the southern Sudan. The initial six months of Lifeline averted another famine; food scarcity, together with the war, had claimed some 250,000 victims the previous year.

Despite the pleas of Sudanese relief groups to use their agreement as the foundation for a broader peace agreement, no sustained efforts were made to bring the war to a halt. Recalled the late UNICEF executive director, James P. Grant, there was

43

nothing in his mandate empowering him to do so. Nor did senior officials from the political side of the UN pursue energetic parallel-track negotiations.

Sudan's civil war, rekindled in late 1990, has dragged on since, with the suffering mounting and the belligerents less and less cooperative. Yet there have been no serious diplomatic initiatives to negotiate an end to the war. When a troubleshooter was finally appointed by the UN in 1993, the mandate was not to promote a negotiated settlement to the conflict but rather to negotiate access for humanitarian operations to embattled areas. As a result, humanitarian efforts were increasingly outmatched by fresh war-generated suffering, with aid agencies increasingly in doubt about the appropriateness of continuing to try to assist.

A full five years after the initial breakthrough in gaining access through consent rather than coercion, the bloodletting in Sudan continues. The growing realization of the need for augmented pressure for peace has yet to be translated into effective diplomatic action. As in the former Yugoslavia, providing assistance assumed a dynamic of its own which eclipsed other necessary and related tasks and has led to a new generation of suffering.

▶ **The Case of Cambodia:** Shifting to more positive illustrations, the experience of the UN Transitional Authority in Cambodia (UNTAC) illuminates how separate sets of activities with a common objective can be mutually supportive. The Paris Agreements of October 1991, signed by 19 governments, closed the curtain on two decades of international and civil strife in Cambodia. The UN Security Council gave UNTAC broad authority in foreign affairs, public security, national defense, finance and information. These five tasks, deemed necessary given the prevailing state of chaos and destruction in Cambodia, represented an unprecedented degree of UN intrusiveness in the internal affairs of a country.

To implement its mandate, UNTAC organized its work into seven components: military, civil administration, police, electoral, human rights, repatriation and rehabilitation. At its peak,

44

UNTAC involved some 22,000 personnel, of whom over two thirds were soldiers and military support staff. They worked with Cambodian nationals from early 1992 through the elections in May 1993, when UNTAC was phased out and authority reverted to Cambodian institutions. Some UN personnel remained to assist in specific areas such as rehabilitation and human rights. The UN's humanitarian activities were firmly integrated in the last three of these components. The head of UNTAC repatriation efforts doubled as special representative of the UNHCR.

UNTAC was a multifaceted and largely successful effort to tackle interconnected problems on parallel tracks. In order for some 370,000 civilians to return home voluntarily from camps along the Thai border, security had to be assured and abuses by the Khmer Rouge, who were responsible for the deaths of over a million Cambodians after the Communist victory in 1975, and by other factions prevented. Repatriation needed to be followed promptly by rehabilitation. Some 200,000 soldiers had to be demobilized and given jobs. Almost as many inter-

Under the auspices of UNTAC, Cambodian refugees return home aboard a UNHCR train in August 1992.

nally displaced people required attention. Given the destruction of infrastructure and residual animosities, international personnel had to supervise the basic system of law and order. Elections had to be organized in a neutral political environment where people, many for the first time in their lives, could vote without fear of retribution. Bringing refugees home and helping them resume productive lives, as called for in the Paris accords, came to represent UNTAC's most successful component.

The Cambodian experience suggests the mainly positive interaction between humanitarianism and politics. UNHCR mobilized $128 million to provide those wishing to return with transport, assistance in clearing customs, protection from extortion, counseling about safe areas, help in family reunification and transitional assistance in the form of food, cash and land—one of the most ambitious population movements ever organized by UNHCR. UN peacekeeping troops added an element of safety, and the presence of other UN and international personnel provided additional security at the local level. Humanitarian activities thus benefited from the political track.

The converse was also true. The decisions of Cambodians to return home and their success in doing so safely buoyed the peace process. Humanitarian efforts contributed to confidence-building in local communities, where people eventually overcame their justifiable fears and went to the polls. The presence of UN Volunteers, stationed in the hinterlands as election supervisors and human-rights monitors, was essential in encouraging people to exercise their franchise.

Moreover, while the patterns of resettlement were voluntary, UNHCR worked to assure that refugees from camps controlled by a given faction on the Thai border did not necessarily return to territories controlled by the same faction in Cambodia. In a highly politicized situation in which each of the four factions sought to control "its" civilian population and outside aid, UNHCR helped defuse factionalism and open areas to international presence and accountability. Thus it accelerated the reconciliation process and benefited the entire UNTAC operation.

To be sure, there were problems, as should be expected in the aftermath of decades of bitter civil war. Delays in deploying UN troops and a lack of UN assertiveness vis-à-vis the Khmer Rouge had serious humanitarian consequences. UN unwillingness to insist that the Cambodian authorities address human-rights abuses allowed violations to go uncontested. Snail's-pace removal of land mines contributed to a shortage of arable land, a buildup of social tensions and economic insecurity, and deaths and serious injuries among those who tried to demine fields on their own. The decision by governments to defer serious reconstruction until after the elections had serious political and humanitarian fallout. Yet these problems themselves confirmed the positive potential of parallel-track strategies and the dangers of proceeding otherwise.

▶ **The Case of El Salvador:** A final country illustration, the most positive of all four, is drawn from El Salvador. The UN brokered an end to the conflict between the government and the insurgents and established a multifaceted operation less intrusive than that in Cambodia. The UN did not attempt to take over important domestic ministries or deploy substantial military forces. However, as with UNTAC, the UN Observer Mission in El Salvador (ONUSAL) did mount humanitarian and political activities on parallel tracks. The initiative was generally successful on both tracks, each benefiting from the other. In fact, ONUSAL was sufficiently well established by early 1992 to serve as a model for UNTAC.

The UN Security Council established ONUSAL in May 1991, at a time when the UN was playing a role in peace negotiations between the Salvadoran government and the insurgent Farabundo Martí National Liberation Front (FMLN). Monitoring the human-rights performance of both sides before the belligerents had agreed to a cease-fire contributed to confidence in, and the momentum of, negotiations. ONUSAL's duties expanded considerably in February 1992 with the actual negotiating and then implementing of a cease-fire. Its provisions called for disengaging the belligerents, disarming the FMLN, monitoring human-rights violations and removing other

47

obstacles that had kept the belligerents apart for a decade. The cease-fire also worked to establish law and order, provided for the training of persons to help preserve it, and introduced greater equity in government institutions and services.

Once again, the diverse members of the UN's humanitarian family were an integral part of a broader political undertaking. Agencies such as UNHCR, WFP and UNICEF had already been providing assistance for some time in both government- and insurgent-held areas. By contributing to a climate of growing confidence between the belligerents, they eased the way for the UN's diplomatic efforts. After the war, a UNHCR initiative to replace the missing papers of refugees, displaced persons and others whose documentation had been lost helped reinvigorate civil society.

Conversely, humanitarian activities benefited from the overall momentum generated by ONUSAL, which provided a framework within which national reconstruction and reconciliation could at last be pursued. After a decade in which 75,000 had died at the hands of right- and left-wing death squads, ONUSAL's reporting of abuses underscored the importance of protecting human rights. It laid the groundwork for a national Truth Commission that courageously required accountability from senior wartime violators of human rights. ONUSAL also helped mayors return to municipalities in conflict zones and achieved recognition for community groups—some of them suspect for their wartime activities—who wished to play a role in reconstruction. The presence of some 600 ONUSAL-associated international personnel had important practical and symbolic benefits for postwar reconstruction and reconciliation.

As with UNTAC, however, there were some rough edges in relationships between humanitarian and political players. Frictions developed between UN officials with a short-term and essentially political mandate and their colleagues on the humanitarian and development side whose responsibilities required a longer-term involvement. Thus the UN secretary-general, in the interest of easing the immediate financial and other burdens on the Salvadoran government, overruled the recommendations of the UNDP and the Food and Agriculture Organization (FAO) regarding the scale and pace of land transfers to returning refugees. As in Cambodia, the politically driven calendar for concluding as quickly as possible the UN peacekeeping operation meant that action on long-standing problems identified by aid personnel was deferred. These remained to be addressed by humanitarian and development agencies after UN soldiers and political emissaries had departed.

In a variety of ways, ONUSAL was more effective than UNTAC. One major difference was that the warring parties in El Salvador were more fatigued by a prolonged stalemate and hence readier to agree on a cease-fire and to make it work. The involvement of the UN secretary-general himself in the peace process from the outset helped speed the arrival of personnel for ONUSAL: the first elements arrived to monitor human rights even before the peace agreement had been finalized. Moreover, El Salvador was geographically smaller than Cambodia, much of its governmental infrastructure was more or less intact and it required less outside assistance.

The Salvadoran experience with the positive and reinforcing aspects of humanitarian and political action was not unique in the region. In a dozen years, beginning in 1981, more than 10 percent of Central America's 18 million people were displaced by war. In addition to the 75,000 Salvadorans, some 30,000 Nicaraguans and 100,000 Guatemalans lost their lives. In spite of setbacks and tensions, humanitarian concerns provided an important impetus to diplomatic action and themselves benefited from regional and international political efforts to end the armed conflicts.

Conclusions

From this review of four examples of parallel-track approaches, several conclusions emerge. First, humanitarian activities have positive political potential. Effectively managed, they can promote a sense of normalcy and contribute to a climate of reconciliation. The safe and well-organized return of people from the Thai border to Cambodia represented a positive beginning for the task of social reconstruction. So, too, the orderly reincorporation of displaced people into El Salvador helped that country turn the corner after a decade of violence.

Progress on the political side can also benefit humanitarian efforts. The success of international mediation in Cambodia and El Salvador placed substantial outside resources in the service of those displaced by each war. Successful mediation helped create a climate in which economic and social reconstruction became a feasible part of the working agenda. A sound political strategy thus contributes to—even though it does not guarantee—success in the humanitarian arena. International political interest can support and reinforce positive changes at the national and community level.

On the other hand, humanitarian activities pursued in a political vacuum can be counterproductive. Aid efforts in the former Yugoslavia and in Sudan, in the absence of serious and effective strategies to end the conflicts, ran into overpowering obstacles. The assurance of continued humanitarian assistance under virtually any conditions relieves the pressure on political and military decisionmakers to end wars. Political strategies undertaken without attention to their humanitarian impact, as in Haiti, can have disastrous results. Although the elected regime was ultimately restored, economic sanctions themselves did not persuade the military junta to leave; rather, sanctions spurred the flight of people by boat and deepened the suffering of those who remained.

The relationships between humanitarian and political action are thus complex. Frequently options are limited and effects difficult to anticipate. Using economic or military coercion to send a political message can wreak havoc. At the same time, the continuous provision of humanitarian aid, no questions asked, can sustain inhumane politics and permit war to be pursued with impunity.

This review of recent experience suggests that humanitarian and political actions need to be conceived and implemented on parallel tracks, each reinforcing but not preempting the other. Neither humanitarian nor political action is sufficient in itself; both are necessary. Absorbed as part of a political strategy, humanitarian action may suffer. Devoid of humane values, political action can precipitate a humanitarian disaster. Political action benefits from making space for humanitarian action; humane values require supportive politics to sustain them.

Key to Abbreviations

AID:	U.S. Agency for International Development
CIA:	Central Intelligence Agency
DHA:	Department of Humanitarian Affairs
FAO:	Food and Agriculture Organization
FMLN:	Farabundo Martí National Liberation Front
ICRC:	International Committee of the Red Cross
IRC:	International Rescue Committee
NATO:	North Atlantic Treaty Organization
NGO:	Nongovernmental organization
OECD:	Organization for Economic Cooperation and Development
ONUSAL:	UN Observer Mission in El Salvador
PDD:	Presidential Decision Directive
UNDP:	UN Development Program
UNHCR:	UN High Commissioner for Refugees
UNICEF:	UN Children's Fund
UNTAC:	UN Transitional Authority in Cambodia
WFP:	World Food Program

4

Looking to the Future

During the cold war, human needs were viewed in
the light of East-West allegiances and often went
unattended in major parts of the globe. When they did receive
attention, the motivation was often political. Solidarity across
ideological lines was rare. The post-cold-war era is a propitious
time to move human values from the periphery to the center of
the global agenda.

In this respect, the new approach of the UN Security Council is welcome. The world's highest political body now treats
life-threatening suffering as a potential threat to international
peace and security. But it still sees human needs through
political lenses and is selective in the suffering that it chooses
to address. In targeting economic sanctions, for example, why
the former Yugoslavia and not Sudan? In mounting military
action, why northern Iraq and not Rwanda?

The humanitarian imperative requires asserting and defend-
ing humane values everywhere as important in their own right.

The denial of food, humanitarian access, or other basic rights anywhere represents a direct challenge to the international community's ethical foundations. They deserve attention whether or not international peace and security are threatened, a subjective and quintessential political determination.

A humanitarian politics that puts human beings at the center is beginning to emerge from the rubble of the cold war and from recent events. Intervention by the international community in Iraq and Somalia without the consent of governments conveys a new message about the evolving balance between sovereignty and solidarity: use sovereignty responsibly or you may lose it altogether.

In June 1993, this new humanitarian politics was articulated at the World Conference on Human Rights in Vienna, Austria. The setting was a contentious one, the first major conference in decades to deal with the highly charged issue of human rights. Some developing countries, from the Middle East and Asia in particular, questioned the universality of human rights and the preoccupation of Western countries with individual and political rights. Developed countries, for their part, had difficulty with the insistence of poorer nations on the centrality of social and economic rights to a meaningful concept of human dignity.

UN Secretary General Boutros-Ghali made an eloquent case for human rights of both sorts. "Human rights," he affirmed, are universal and "the ultimate norm of all politics." Yet he also reminded those present of the importance of "rights of solidarity." These collective rights, embraced by the UN General Assembly and international legal covenants, include "the right to a healthy environment, the right to peace, the right to food security, the right to ownership of the common heritage of mankind, and, above all, the right to development."

Humanitarian politics needs to capitalize on the heightened international concern for protecting human rights. But how should that concern be conceived and acted upon? "The single most policy- and thought-befuddling issue of the post-cold-war '90s," wrote Stephen Rosenfeld in *The Washington Post* in February 1994, "is whether the Bosnias, Somalias and Haitis are so important to the United States that we should be prepared to intervene to shape an outcome to our liking or whether we can live well enough with whatever result emerges on its own."

Those who argue that what happens in the world's remote trouble spots is of no direct consequence to the United States have a certain persuasiveness. Their case is reinforced by the fact that the world has done poorly in moderating the worst aspects of recent crises, whether headline-grabbing emergencies or the more quiet degradation of year-in, year-out poverty and powerlessness. Moreover, the highly localized and particularistic causes of many of today's conflicts seriously limit what the United States or other powerful outsider nations can do.

Protecting principles—political no less than humanitarian—has indeed proved perilous. Reviewing the world's failure to resist aggression in the former Yugoslavia, the British academic Jonathan Eyal observed to a *New York Times* reporter: "We should give up the obscene idea of keeping Bosnia-Herzegovina together, accept the country's outright division, and admit that we have no more principles to defend." This counsel of despair is unacceptable.

A Global Vision

Rather than cynicism, what is required is a new sense of global politics in which human welfare and human rights become, in the UN secretary-general's words, the norm. With humankind at the center of humanitarian politics, narrow concepts of the national interest of individual states are replaced by a more inclusive vision of global welfare, not just next door or across the country but around the globe.

This is in fact the theme of the recent report by The Commission on Global Governance, entitled *Our Global Neighborhood*. The commission notes: "Even in 1945, few could envision the world as one neighborhood. But the changes of the last half century have begun to transform the incipient global neighborhood into a reality."

Thus, the destruction of Dubrovnik, Sarajevo and Mostar

represents a tragedy not only for the three cities in the former Yugoslavia and their inhabitants. Their ruin is a threat to the widely cherished principle that people of diverse religious and ethnic backgrounds can live together and enrich one another's lives. The savaging of Somali civilians by warlords and their henchmen is an affront to all who affirm the universal right to food and the preciousness of human life. The butchery in Rwanda is an assault against human decency that cheapens the quality of life everywhere.

Putting concern for people at the top of the agenda requires not only insisting that warring parties assume responsibilities for their violations of humanity. It also means acting to stem abuses and infuse international and domestic political life with a greater sense of humanity. "The problem is not of morality versus politics," the Independent Commission on International Humanitarian Issues noted, "but rather of the kind of politics which allow moral restraints to emerge and to be observed." In short, more effective political strategies must be found to reinforce humanitarian concerns.

Institutional Implications

How does the world get there from here? Effective humanitarian politics requires some major changes in current practices.

▶ First, within the UN, a better balance is required between the humanitarian and political sides of the organization. As a step in that direction, the Security Council should be required to review major humanitarian crises once they have reached a stated magnitude; at present the council can choose to ignore an issue until it is too late. The council should also be required, before acting on a given crisis, to solicit the views of UN humanitarian organizations and take into account the likely humanitarian consequences of its actions. That might mean changing the proposed course of action because the consequences for civilian populations (for example, an economic embargo against Haiti) would be too severe. It might mean that the council or its member governments would commit themselves in advance to underwrite fully the costs of compensating for such consequences (UN sanctions against Serbia are a case in point).

Where humanitarian activities are part of multifunctional UN peacekeeping operations, a more proportional allocation of funds and personnel for humanitarian functions should be required (as in the case of Cambodia). An upgrading of the importance of humanitarian concerns is necessary in order for the Department of Humanitarian Affairs, currently the weak leg of a three-legged stool, to enjoy influence comparable to that associated with the Departments of Political Affairs and Peacekeeping Operations.

The UN's humanitarian work may also require insulation from the effects of the UN's political actions. As a UN policy statement points out, "humanitarian and political objectives do not necessarily coincide." As a result, the statement continues, UN humanitarian agencies should be encouraged to "maintain a certain degree of independence from UN-authorized political and/or military activities."

This safeguard would deny the Security Council and the secretary-general operational control over UN humanitarian programs and help preserve distinctions in UN operations between UN humanitarian and military-political personnel. In some circumstances, the independence of UN humanitarian action may be more important than the coordination of all UN activities, political and humanitarian.

▶ Second, major changes are required inside the UN humanitarian apparatus itself. The division of labor among such agencies as UNICEF, WFP, UNHCR and the UN Center for Human Rights is neither clear nor effective. Despite heroic efforts under fire on the front lines by their staffs, these agencies themselves concede that individual organizations and the UN apparatus as a whole must do better.

▶ Third, the UN and non-UN humanitarian actors need to collaborate more creatively. If political constraints prevent UN agencies—as creatures of governments—from reaching distressed populations in areas of conflict or from challenging abusive human-rights policies, NGOs and the ICRC should be called upon to play an expanded role. In most instances, greater collegiality and collaboration among the entire family of agencies are possible and desirable.

A special area of potential collaboration concerns the military, who in recent crises have played direct as well as contributory humanitarian roles. A number of ideas deserve review. One would be to form within the ranks of UN peacekeeping forces a humanitarian contingent that would relieve the UN's civilian agencies from providing lifesaving assistance in the heat of battle. This option may be particularly attractive in active war zones when UN peacekeeping forces are present without the consent of the belligerents. Another idea would be to create a UN humanitarian security police force comprised of armed civilians, independent of UN peacekeeping troops, who would protect humanitarian operations and personnel.

▶ Fourth, effective humanitarian politics will require firmer and more principled support from governments. Governments underwrite most of the financing for humanitarian operations, whether carried out by themselves or by the UN, NGOs or the ICRC. Governments also provide political support for such work through the UN Security Council and the governing bodies of the various UN organizations and through their relationships with private humanitarian bodies.

Government contributions to the world organization have not kept pace with the skyrocketing costs of humanitarian and peacekeeping activities. The United States is the UN's largest debtor, with unmet obligations in mid-1994 totaling some $1.3 billion. In UN Security Council discussions in 1993 on a possible initiative to respond to a crisis in Burundi, for example, Washington announced that it would not contribute to such an operation and even tried to prevent other governments from launching it. The United States would have been obligated to pay over 30 percent of the bill, according to the UN's assessment formula, and might have been drawn into the action in other ways as well.

Here, again, fundamental policy issues require review. What

can be done to promote more equitable burden-sharing among governments? Will greater financial contributions by a wider range of countries necessitate changes in the current makeup of the Security Council? Can humanitarian activities achieve their proper prominence as long as they are funded by "voluntary contributions," while governments are "assessed" their fair share of peacekeeping costs? How can governments that have had a history of pressing the UN into the service of their own agendas be encouraged to take a more principled and consistent approach?

▶ Fifth, any new approach to humanitarian action that puts at the center people rather than politics requires greater respect for those affected by crises and for their own local institutions as effective problem-solvers. More creative ways must be found to make fuller use of local capabilities. Although in crisis after crisis, the local citizenry and institutions provided a first line of defense, the humanitarian system is driven largely by donors and other forces outside the countries and communities in distress. Although outside experts may bring with them know-how, contacts and authority over resources, they often lack insight into the particular conditions governing a given emergency. The financial costs of their involvement and their recommendations are often excessive and inappropriate, particularly in view of expertise available locally.

The involvement of the local citizenry also has a political rationale. Humanitarian crises—particularly those that are not natural disasters but are caused by conflicts—usually occur in communities or among populations largely powerless to prevent them. Since recurrent crises may increase people's vulnerability, outside resources should be made available in ways that enhance their control over their own lives and futures. Experience also demonstrates a correlation between success and local involvement.

▶ Sixth, major humanitarian crises are not isolated sets of events that lend themselves to resolution through quick responses with specific sets of inputs. Rather, they are stages in the evolution of societies with complex histories and intercom-

munal dynamics. Theorists and practitioners are now in broad agreement regarding the requirement to connect emergency action to prevention, on the one hand, and to development efforts, on the other.

Recent crises have been foreshadowed by warnings: increasingly strident political discourse, a pattern of human-rights abuses, a stockpiling of weapons and ammunition, unusual movements of populations. The genocide unleashed in Rwanda within a few hours of the downing in April 1994 of a presidential aircraft was carefully planned in advance. Nipping such crises in the bud would be much more cost-effective and more humane than responding after the fact. Preventing them altogether, either through more effective development strategies or advance troop deployments, would be better yet. Viewing relief as an investment in reconstruction and as a step toward longer-term development also makes eminently good sense.

A New Generation of Humanitarians

Responding effectively to crises caused largely by human action requires a new degree of professionalism among practitioners. While responding from the heart has always been their trademark, functioning in today's civil wars necessitates at least an equal portion of tough-mindedness. Commenting on the kind of aid personnel required to cope with the Rwandan tragedy, Johanna Grombach, who headed the ICRC's 30-member team in the refugee camp in Goma, Zaire, observed, "They shouldn't have too great a heart. If you want to save the world, forget it. We don't need people who are too empathetic. We need professionals."

Caught in crossfire in earlier wars, humanitarian personnel are now themselves the specific targets of warring parties; humanitarian insignias no longer afford protection. Moreover, aid personnel formerly responded to specific life-and-death crises within still-functioning countries. Today such crises are not only more multifaceted but can lead to, or reflect, the collapse of entire states. Emergency responses represent but one element in the complex process of conflict resolution and social, economic and political reconstruction.

Aid agencies that have prided themselves on being apolitical now face situations that are, by their very nature, political. Humanitarian actions can affect the balance of power in already highly politicized situations. Neutrality thus requires enormous political savvy. In fact, some organizations are questioning whether neutrality should even remain a goal. They prefer to acknowledge that their activities—for example, expressing solidarity with those who suffer and seeking a balance among the warring parties—have political repercussions.

Such formidable challenges have stimulated humanitarian organizations to review their terms of engagement. A number of individual agencies have recently amended their policies and operational procedures. Several codes of conduct are currently being developed by clusters of humanitarian groups. Military professionals and others engaged in peacekeeping work are also writing new ground rules and training manuals.

Finally, a better informed constituency is required to support and underwrite humanitarian activities. Each of the major actors has its own particular base of support: the UN looks to member states, donor governments to congresses or parliaments, and NGOs to private contributors. The support provided, both financial and political, to make programs possible may also either encourage or discourage risk‚taking. The complexity of the issues, and the need for pairing emergency action with longer-term change, necessitates more knowledgeable supporters.

Challenges of Civil Wars

As the balance between sovereignty and solidarity evolves and the humanitarian compact is rewritten, the challenges of mounting effective action in civil wars are becoming more arduous. When governments have difficulty striking the right balance, constituencies lose heart. When chaos returns following an expensive intervention, as in Somalia, it is easy to come to the conclusion that the mistake the world made was in seeking to help rather than in the ways it went about doing so.

When relief is implicated in the continuation of conflict, as in Sudan, humanitarian organizations require support for toughening their approach or, as a last resort, for suspending operations altogether. When, as in Bosnia-Herzegovina, the suspension of activities is likely to create more suffering than their continuation will alleviate, support is required so that agencies stay the course. Greater discernment on the part of humanitarian professionals facing such tough judgments should be matched by better informed and more durable constituencies.

Those who support humanitarian action in such trying circumstances will quite properly demand greater accountability of the organizations that act on their behalf. Contributors, whether in congresses or pews, legitimately ask whether initiatives are cost-effective, whether duplication among agencies is creative or counterproductive, whether emergency aid is laying the groundwork for longer-term changes, whether short-term gains are offset by longer-term problems. The intended beneficiaries of humanitarian action demand—and deserve—a more pivotal role in accountability as well.

5

Implications for U.S. Policy

RESPONDING TO the life-threatening suffering of the post-cold-war era is a challenge to the entire international community and all of its public and private humanitarian institutions. Because of its historical leadership role among developed countries and its status as sole remaining superpower, the United States is indisputably the preeminent actor among governments.

Reflecting U.S. status as a permanent member of the UN Security Council and the largest contributor to the UN, American influence in the world body remains powerful, though less controlling than in the past. A substantial investor in NGOs and the ICRC, the United States also plays a key role in shaping their work. American troops, rarely and only reluctantly under UN command, have nevertheless been key humanitarian actors in multinational undertakings in northern Iraq, Somalia and Haiti. In fact, it is logistically and politically unlikely that a major international humanitarian operation would be undertaken without strong American participation or encouragement.

The current spate of humanitarian crises, and others that will surely follow, have four major implications for U.S. policy.

More Active Support for Multilateral Initiatives

In the Persian Gulf crisis of 1990–91, many criticized the strong-arm tactics that the United States employed to produce a Security Council vote in support of military intervention against Iraq. The United States and the UN had not moved with equal dispatch, they pointed out, to implement other Security Council resolutions (for example, regarding Israeli withdrawal from the occupied territories). The United States also drew fire in 1991 for suspending bilateral economic aid to Yemen, some of it channeled through American NGOs, in retaliation for its failure to support the U.S. position in the Security Council. Critics charged that the United States was using the UN to advance an American agenda while reneging on its financial obligations.

Four years and numerous crises later, the United States is still the single most influential government among UN members and remains the deepest in debt to the organization. As of mid-1994, the United States owed $748 million of the total $2.5 billion in peacekeeping arrearages and $530 million of the total $830 million of unpaid dues for the regular UN budget.

In August 1994, the Congress passed an appropriation bill that would allow payment in full of outstanding U.S. peacekeeping debts. This represented a major step in restoring the U.S. image as a country that respects its international commitments. Yet the Congress was unwilling to provide another $300 million—the Administration had suggested that the sum be drawn from the Defense Department budget—to underwrite UN peace enforcement initiatives undertaken with U.S. consent. It also did not appropriate enough to pay U.S. arrearages to the regular UN budget and those of various UN organizations, which will not be satisfied until 1997 at the earliest.

Clearly if Washington expects the UN to undertake urgent

international action of importance to the United States (as in the Persian Gulf war or in Haiti), it must meet its financial obligations. Moreover, the strategy of keeping the UN on a short leash by manipulating U.S. financial contributions is a violation of U.S. treaty obligations and undermines the American insistence that other states take their own duties seriously.

Steadier Leadership, More Consistent Policies

A related challenge concerns the quality of American leadership in the humanitarian sphere. The United States prides itself on being the world's most generous aid donor and on providing outstanding leadership to the UN for a half century. U.S. NGOs, for their part, with broad support from the American people, have traditionally responded promptly and fulsomely to international crises.

In recent years, U.S. leadership has slipped. Tokyo has outdistanced Washington in the aggregate amount of economic assistance provided to developing countries. For decades, the Nordic countries and the Netherlands have devoted a higher percentage of their respective gross national products than the United States to official development assistance and a larger share to basic human needs.

Moreover, American humanitarian aid policy has lacked consistency. The United States vacillated in its approach to the Haitian military regime, the reinstatement of the elected president, the enforcement of sanctions, and the treatment of people who fled. Washington's policy toward the conflict in the former Yugoslavia has also fluctuated, for example, with respect to using NATO air strikes against the Bosnian Serb army or lifting the arms embargo against the Bosnian government. The United States has encouraged others but has not itself been willing to provide ground troops to protect humanitarian convoys. After committing U.S. troops to Somalia, it abruptly decided to withdraw them.

The damage caused by such vacillation has been considerable. Officials in the UN and in other key governments, to say nothing of belligerents in the conflict areas themselves, have been confused about U.S. intentions. The American people themselves have not had a clear sense of what their government was seeking to accomplish and how.

Consistency is particularly important in major crises when the influence of the United States is pivotal in fashioning the world's response. In circumstances that call for the UN to assume operational and financial responsibilities, American concurrence is essential for the world organization's undertakings to succeed. In other situations where governments seek the UN's blessing before proceeding—for example, as France did before sending a mission to Rwanda—U.S. acquiescence rather than support may be adequate.

While Washington may properly withhold its support from certain UN undertakings, it needs to avoid blocking initiatives by other countries in response to major emergencies. Acquiescing to actions about which it is less than enthusiastic is one of the costs of multilateralism. The days are past when the United States can expect the rest of the world to do its bidding.

Early indications are that the 104th Congress, however, is more disposed to emphasize the costs to the United States rather than the benefits of multilateral cooperation. Such retrenchment in U.S. policy is often explained as motivated by a desire for greater "burden-sharing" by other nations. In reality, however, the United States itself is increasingly the burden for other countries and the UN.

A Broader View of National Interests

Contributing to the inconsistency of U.S. humanitarian aid policy is a lack of consensus about the nature of national interests. Gone is the clarity of the cold-war era when advances in communism anywhere were perceived as a direct threat to the United States. Post-cold-war policy is influenced instead by many and shifting factors—geographical proximity, commercial considerations, global standing, media attention and domestic constituencies—factors that vary from one crisis to the next, and sometimes from one moment to the next.

The first application of the aforementioned Presidential

Decision Directive 25 resulted in the U.S. refusal to act miltarily in the face of a massive humanitarian catastrophe in Rwanda. Officials even banned the term genocide, realizing that acknowledging that genocide was taking place would create legal obligations for action. Finally, three months after the bloodletting began, with a tenth of Rwanda's population dead and half of those who remained displaced by violence, the Administration reversed itself and committed troops to help with the Rwandan refugees in Zaire. The cost of the response vastly exceeded the probable cost of intervening earlier.

What had changed between the beginning of genocide in April and the arrival of troops in August was not U.S. interests but Washington's perception of them. The insistence that every U.S. undertaking directly benefit the American people—the lesson apparently distilled from Somalia and Bosnia and spelled out in PDD 25—puts a straitjacket on U.S. policy. It distorts perceptions of global challenges, shortchanges American interest in stability and undermines respect for international law.

What is needed instead is to understand the U.S. national interests more broadly, encompassing enduring American values such as long-standing humanitarian traditions. "We need to define national interest in the post-cold-war world," observes Andrew Natsios, formerly head of the U.S. government's Office of Foreign Disaster Assistance and currently an NGO official, "to include complex emergencies even when there is no geostrategic interest." In this broader context, the United States stands to benefit from, and should contribute appropriately to, a better functioning and more universal international humanitarian safety net.

Greater Constituency Awareness

If, as Ambrose Bierce is reported to have said, "wars are God's way of teaching Americans geography," recent humanitarian crises are a continuation of the same seminar. In terms of humanitarian and political literacy, the United States has considerable catching up to do. Canada, the Nordic countries and the Netherlands have routinely and generously contributed personnel and funds for UN peacekeeping activities and for the UN's humanitarian agencies. That fact reflects a better informed public in those nations and greater public awareness than exists in the United States of the importance of such activities not only to the victims but also to the providers of the assistance. That awareness is the fruit of determined educational efforts for generations by their governments and NGOs.

Nurturing a more knowledgeable constituency is a challenge for both the U.S. government and American NGOs. Modest funding from a wide variety of official sources, including AID and the U.S. Department of Education, is available, but should be given out with fewer strings. The Administration's foreign policy will garner more enthusiastic support among the American people to the extent that human beings are more clearly at its center. The media could also play an expanded role in promoting greater international literacy among Americans.

If humanitarianism is to be less simplistic, U.S. NGOs must see their own tasks in a broader political context, curtail self-promotion, and be less preoccupied with guarding their turf. Educating constituencies and advocating humanitarian politics should become priorities.

Talking It Over

A Note for Students and Discussion Groups

This issue of the HEADLINE SERIES, like its predecessors, is published for every serious reader, specialized or not, who takes an interest in the subject. Many of our readers will be in classrooms, seminars or community discussion groups. Particularly with them in mind, we present below some discussion questions—suggested as a starting point only—and references for further reading.

Discussion Questions

Select a recent humanitarian crisis and analyze the way the world responded. How effective was the response? Was the relationship between humanitarianism and politics about right?

International law affirms the right to humanitarian assistance. Humanitarian organizations are expected to provide such assistance without political, religious or other strings. Is it politically naïve to expect UN agencies, U.S. AID, or private relief groups to function in that manner?

The existing humanitarian assistance system does not now respond to all instances of life-threatening suffering. Should the world commit itself to a system that addresses all such crises? Until one is in place, what criteria should determine which of the many emergencies receive priority?

Humanitarian organizations differ about whether to integrate their activities fully into, or insulate themselves thoroughly from, UN politico-military undertakings. A third approach would have only a special corps of aid agencies involved when a UN embargo has been imposed or UN troops are enforcing a peace agreement. Which of the three approaches makes the most sense to you?

What are your views on using military force to protect or assist humanitarian activities? Would you support the use of greater force than is presently applied to counteract warring parties that deny access to civilians in life-threatening situations?

Sovereignty has been the bedrock of international relations and of the UN Charter. Have recent efforts to ensure humanitarian access to civilians inside national borders altered the common notion of sovereignty and domestic jurisdiction?

Among the codes of conduct currently under discussion are the Providence Principles, printed on page 18. How appropriate and feasible do these ground rules seem to you?

Given the prevailing understanding of humanitarian action as pristine and principled and politics as dirty and compromise-laden, is the concept of humanitarian politics a helpful one?

Annotated Reading List

Anderson, Mary B., and Woodrow, Peter J., *Rising from the Ashes: Development Strategies in Times of Disaster.* Boulder, Colo., Westview Press, 1989. Case studies of emergency relief and links to rebuilding and development.

Boutros-Ghali, Boutros, *An Agenda for Peace: Preventive Diplomacy, Peacemaking and Peace-keeping.* New York, United Nations, 1992. A broad-ranging policy statement by the UN secretary-general that is likely to frame discussion of political and humanitarian issues for some time.

Brown, Michael E., ed., *Ethnic Conflict and International Security.* Princeton, N.J., Princeton University Press, 1993. Essays on various dimensions of the security crises of the 1990s.

Childers, Erskine, with Urquhart, Brian, *Renewing the United Nations System.* Uppsala, Sweden, Dag Hammarskjöld Foundation, 1994. A recent and comprehensive proposal for UN reform by two UN veterans.

Damrosch, Lori Fisler, ed., *Enforcing Restraint: Collective Intervention in Internal Conflicts.* New York, Council on Foreign Relations, 1993. Case studies of outside involvement in the civil wars of the early post-cold-war era.

Deng, Francis M., *Protecting the Dispossessed: A Challenge for the International Community.* Washington, D.C., Brookings Institution, 1993. First-person narrative by the UN secretary-general's special representative about the problems of persons displaced within their own countries.

Donnelly, Jack, *International Human Rights.* Boulder, Colo., Westview Press, 1993. An introduction to international human rights.

Gregg, Robert W., *About Face?: The United States and the United Nations.* Boulder, Colo., Lynne Rienner, 1993. An analysis of the tumultuous U.S. policy reversals of the 1980s.

Loescher, Gil, *Beyond Charity: International Cooperation and the Global Refugee Crisis.* New York, Oxford University Press, 1993. A discussion of the governmental, intergovernmental and nongovernmental structures that have evolved to cope with the ever-growing number of refugees.

Minear, Larry, and Weiss, Thomas G., *Mercy Under Fire: War and the Global Humanitarian Community.* Boulder, Colo., Westview Press, 1995. The lessons of humanitarian action in armed conflicts in the post-cold-war era.

Roberts, Adam, and Kingsbury, Benedict, eds., *United Nations, Divided World: The UN's Roles in International Relations,* 2nd ed. New York, Oxford University Press, 1993. Scholars and practitioners examine the UN's efforts in the post-cold-war era in light of historical developments.

United Nations High Commissioner for Refugees, *The State of the World's Refugees, 1993: The Challenge of Protection.* New York, Penguin, 1993. Comprehensive data and analysis regarding the world's refugees and internally displaced persons.

Weiss, Thomas G., Forsythe, David P., and Coate, Roger A., *The United Nations and Changing World Politics.* Boulder, Colo., Westview Press, 1994. An up-to-date treatment of the world organization's political, legal and operational activities.